THE COMMONWEALTH GAMES

Nick Hunter

Raintree is an imprint of Capstone Global Library Limited, a company incorporated in England and Wales having its registered office at 7 Pilgrim Street, London, EC4V 6LB – Registered company number: 6695582

To contact Raintree, please phone 0845 6044371, fax +44 (0)1865 312263, or email: myorders@raintreepublishers.co.uk.

Edited by Nick Hunter and Diyan Leake
Designed by Steve Mead
Original illustrations © Capstone Global Library Ltd 2014
Picture research by Ruth Blair
Production by Victoria Fitzgerald
Originated by Capstone Global Library Ltd
Printed in China by CTPS

ISBN 978 1 406 26172 1 (hardback)
17 16 15 14 13
10 9 8 7 6 5 4 3 2 1

ISBN 978 1 406 26174 5 (paperback)
17 16 15 14 13
10 9 8 7 6 5 4 3 2 1

British Library Cataloguing in Publication Data
Hunter, Nick
The Commonwealth Games.
A full catalogue record for this book is available from the British Library.

Acknowledgements
We would like to thank the following for permission to reproduce photographs: The Burlington Historical Society (Ontario, Canada) p. 8; Corbis pp. 6 (© Will Burgess/Reuters), 14 (© Wu Wei/Xinhua Press); Getty Images pp. 4 (Scott Barbour), 5 (Streeter Lecka), 9 (Sydney Morning Herald/Fairfax Media), 10 (Manan Vatsyayana/AFP), 11 (Mike Powell), 12 (Daniel Berehulak), 13 (Matt Dunham/WPAPool), 15 (Mark Dadswell), 16 (William West/AFP), 17 (Graham Crouch), 18 (Cameron Spencer), 19 (Mark Kolbe), 20 (Prakash Singh/AFP), 21 (William West/AFP), 22 (Matt King), 23 (Stu Forster), 24 (Bryn Lennon), 25 (Gary M. Prior), 26 (Jeff J. Mitchell); Shutterstock p. 27 (© Claudio Divizia).

Cover photograph of Peter Mitchell of England, Azizulhasni Awang of Malaysia, Ross Edgar of Scotland, Njisane Phillip of Trinidad & Tobago, Shane Perkins of Australia, and Amrit Singh of India competing in the Men's Keirin qualifier during the track cycling event at the Delhi 2010 Commonwealth Games reproduced with permission of Getty Images (Mark Kolbe).

Every effort has been made to contact copyright holders of material reproduced in this book. Any omissions will be rectified in subsequent printings if notice is given to the publisher.

Contents

Some words are shown in bold, **like this**. You can find out what they mean by looking in the glossary.

The Friendly Games

The **Commonwealth** Games are one of the world's biggest sporting events. Every four years, athletes from countries around the world meet to test their speed, strength, and skill in sports ranging from athletics to **lawn bowls**.

Some of the Commonwealth Games' most popular sports, such as netball, do not feature at the Olympics.

While some events bring nations together in a spirit of fierce competition, the Commonwealth Games are known as "the Friendly Games". In the past, they have celebrated friendship and sporting success in cities from Auckland, New Zealand to Victoria, Canada.

Glasgow 2014

In 2014, the Commonwealth Games will be coming to Glasgow. Scotland's largest city will play host to 4,500 athletes competing in 17 sports for the honour of being the Commonwealth Champion.

Will Olympic and World Champion heptathlete Jessica Ennis add a Commonwealth Games gold medal to her collection?

COMMONWEALTH GAMES OATH

This **oath** is spoken by one athlete at the start of each Commonwealth Games.

"*We declare that we will take part in the Commonwealth Games in the spirit of true sportsmanship, recognizing the rules which govern them and desirous of participating in them for the honour of our Commonwealth and for the glory of sport.*"

The Commonwealth

The athletes at the Commonwealth Games come from the 54 countries that make up the **Commonwealth.** This is an international organization that includes countries from all the world's continents, representing almost one-third of the planet's population.

Shared history

The countries that make up the Commonwealth are linked by a shared history. Almost all of them were once ruled from Great Britain as part of the British Empire. Since 1949, the countries have been equal members of the Commonwealth.

The countries of the Commonwealth work together to promote **democracy** and to help tackle problems around the world. The friendly Commonwealth Games are at the heart of these aims.

QUEEN ELIZABETH II

Queen Elizabeth is head of the Commonwealth and has a long association with the Games. She is **Patron** of the Commonwealth Games Federation. At every Games, a message from the Queen is brought to the opening ceremony by a relay of runners.

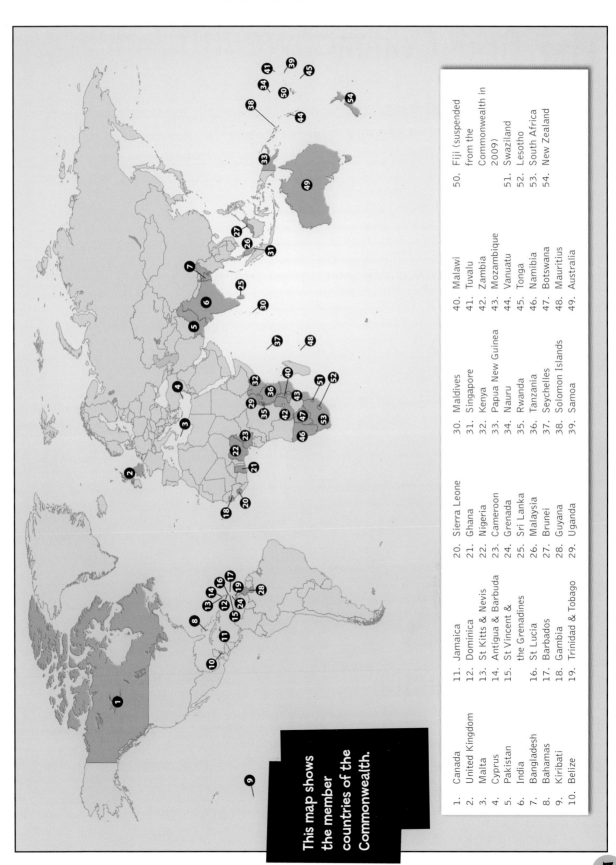

This map shows the member countries of the Commonwealth.

1. Canada
2. United Kingdom
3. Malta
4. Cyprus
5. Pakistan
6. India
7. Bangladesh
8. Bahamas
9. Kiribati
10. Belize
11. Jamaica
12. Dominica
13. St Kitts & Nevis
14. Antigua & Barbuda
15. St Vincent & the Grenadines
16. St Lucia
17. Barbados
18. Gambia
19. Trinidad & Tobago
20. Sierra Leone
21. Ghana
22. Nigeria
23. Cameroon
24. Grenada
25. Sri Lanka
26. Malaysia
27. Brunei
28. Guyana
29. Uganda
30. Maldives
31. Singapore
32. Kenya
33. Papua New Guinea
34. Nauru
35. Rwanda
36. Tanzania
37. Seychelles
38. Solomon Islands
39. Samoa
40. Malawi
41. Tuvalu
42. Zambia
43. Mozambique
44. Vanuatu
45. Tonga
46. Namibia
47. Botswana
48. Mauritius
49. Australia
50. Fiji (suspended from the Commonwealth in 2009)
51. Swaziland
52. Lesotho
53. South Africa
54. New Zealand

The first Commonwealth Games

The first **Commonwealth** Games would not have happened without the efforts of Melville Marks "Bobby" Robinson. Robinson went with the Canadian team to the 1928 Amsterdam Olympic Games. He decided to stage a similar sporting event for the countries of the British Empire.

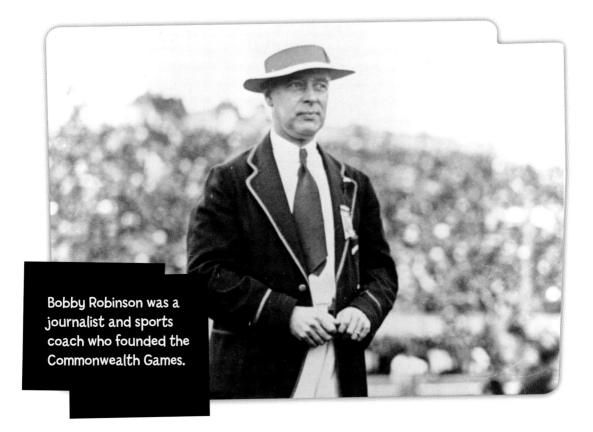

Bobby Robinson was a journalist and sports coach who founded the Commonwealth Games.

Happy Hamilton

The first Commonwealth Games were actually called the British Empire Games and they were held in Robinson's home city of Hamilton, Canada. The world was in the grip of an economic crisis and the city donated $30,000 so athletes could travel to the Games. Although the Games were on a tight **budget**, they were a success. The Friendly Games were born.

COMMONWEALTH FACTFILE:
HAMILTON 1930

- 400 athletes from 11 countries
- Most gold medals: England
- Athletes slept in the Prince of Wales School, next to Hamilton's stadium.

This photo shows the Australian cyclist Bobby Pearce training for the 1930 British Empire Games.

EARLY ATTEMPTS

A sporting festival for the British Empire was first suggested by the Reverend Astley Cooper, writing in 1891. In 1911, athletes from Australia, Canada, South Africa, and the UK competed against each other as part of a Festival of the Empire when King George V came to the throne. However, the festival was never repeated.

The changing Commonwealth Games

The 2010 **Commonwealth** Games in New Delhi, India featured 4,352 athletes from 71 countries competing in 17 sports. They were the biggest Games ever. The Commonwealth Games have come a long way since 1930.

The Games were called the British Empire Games until 1950. But the world was changing and many of the competing countries were becoming **independent**. The name changed, finally becoming the Commonwealth Games for the 1978 event in Edmonton, Canada.

Nigeria's Damola Osayemi lost her gold medal in the women's 100 metres at Delhi when she failed a drugs test.

Commonwealth controversies

The Friendly Games have not always avoided controversy. Political differences have led to some countries refusing to send athletes. Like other sporting events, the Games have also had to deal with athletes cheating by taking drugs to boost their performance.

APARTHEID
South Africa did not attend the Games between 1962 and 1994. Most Commonwealth countries opposed the country's **apartheid** government, which was prejudiced against most of the country's people. In 1986, 32 Commonwealth countries refused to attend the Edinburgh Games because of the British government's weak opposition to apartheid.

South Africa's athletes were welcomed back to the Commonwealth Games family at the 1994 Games in Victoria, Canada.

Symbols and ceremonies

The **Commonwealth** Games begin with a spectacular opening ceremony. The athletes parade through the stadium. In 2014, the parade will be led by India, the host country of the previous Games. Scotland's athletes will appear last in the parade.

The opening ceremony includes music and performances from and about the host city. Delhi's incredible opening ceremony included more than 9,000 performers. The Games are then declared open. One competitor takes the Commonwealth Games **oath** on behalf of all the athletes (see page 5).

Once the Games are open, the official flag for the Games is raised in the stadium.

The closing ceremony is less formal and more of a party for athletes and **volunteers**. One athlete is given the David Dixon Award for their outstanding contribution to the Games. The Games flag is handed on to the next host city.

THE QUEEN'S BATON RELAY

The Relay is a unique feature of the Games. A message from Queen Elizabeth II is carried by a relay of runners across many Commonwealth countries from London to the host city. The message is read out at the opening ceremony.

Queen Elizabeth handed the baton to India's President Prathibha Devi Singh Patil at the start of the 2010 Queen's Baton Relay.

Amazing Africans

The **Commonwealth** Games have yet to be held in Africa, but African countries play an important part in the success of the Games. African nations represented at the Commonwealth Games range from the 150 million people of Nigeria to those from the tiny Seychelles Islands in the Indian Ocean, with less than 100,000 people.

Natalie Du Toit is a legend of the pool. She won seven Commonwealth gold medals in **para-sport** swimming between 2002 and 2010.

Measuring success

The most successful African countries at Delhi 2010 were Kenya and South Africa, with 12 gold medals each. Kenyan athletes have long been the ones to beat in middle and long-distance athletic events. They won an unstoppable 11 gold medals in these events in 2010.

Sierra Leone is one of the world's poorest countries and has been torn apart by war. It has sent athletes to every Commonwealth Games since 1990 without winning a single medal. For many athletes, success comes simply from reaching the Commonwealth Games.

CASTER SEMENYA

Semenya shot to fame when she won the 800 metres race at the World Championships in 2009 at just 18 years old. Having missed the 2010 Commonwealth Games because of injury, the South African will be desperate to add to her 2012 Olympic silver medal at Glasgow 2014.

Boaz Lalang (centre) celebrated winning the 800 metres race at the 2010 Commonwealth Games, finishing just ahead of two other Kenyan athletes.

Asian achievements

India's 1 billion people make up around half the population of the entire **Commonwealth**. India achieved its best ever result when hosting the Games in 2010, finishing second overall in the **medal table** with 39 gold medals.

The Commonwealth Games in Delhi had their fair share of problems. Before the Games, there were concerns that the athletes' village and stadium might not be finished. The head of the organizing committee ended up in jail, accused of **corruption** as the Games cost much more than planned.

India's 4 x 400 metre relay team won the country's first female track gold medal in 2010.

Malaysia and Singapore

Delhi was not the first Commonwealth Games to be held in Asia. That honour went to Kuala Lumpur, Malaysia, in 1998. Malaysia has a long history of success at the Games, particularly in badminton. Singapore's successes also show the range of sports at the Games. The country's 10 gold medals in Delhi came from shooting and table tennis.

Many of the problems of Delhi's games were forgotten once the amazing opening ceremony started.

COMMONWEALTH FACTFILE: DELHI 2010

- 4,352 athletes from 71 countries, competing in 272 events
- Most gold medals: Australia
- Langur monkeys were added to security teams to stop wild monkeys attacking athletes and spectators.

Australia and New Zealand

Australian swimmers and cyclists have led the country to the top of the **medal table** at every Games since 1990. Recent Australian successes also include Steve Hooker's gold in the pole vault and victories in Delhi for both the men's and women's hockey teams.

Australian Anna Meares claimed gold on the track in 2010.

When Queensland's Gold Coast stages the Games in 2018, Australia will have hosted the **Commonwealth** Games more than any other country.

Australia's neighbour New Zealand has been host three times. Team sports were introduced to the Games in 1998 and New Zealand has excelled at netball and **rugby sevens**.

COMMONWEALTH FACTFILE: MELBOURNE 2006

- 4,049 athletes came from 71 countries, competing in 245 events.
- Most gold medals: Australia
- The Queen's Baton Relay visited every country and territory competing before arriving at the Melbourne Cricket Ground for the opening ceremony.

SWIMMING LEGENDS

Australia's dominance has been built on success in the pool, and the exploits of some great swimmers, including:

- Leisel Jones: won 11 gold medals at three Commonwealth Games between 2002 and 2010.
- Susie O'Neill: won 10 swimming gold medals between 1990 and 1998
- Ian Thorpe: won 10 gold medals between 1998 and 2002.

New Zealand's formidable rugby team has won gold at every Games since 1998.

Canada to the Caribbean

Canada is the biggest country in the **Commonwealth**. It has sent a team to every Commonwealth Games since 1930. Canadians have been successful across a whole range of events. Successes at recent Games include Tara Whitten, who won four medals for cycling in Delhi. Also in 2010, athletics coach Carla Nicholls showed the spirit of the Friendly Games when she rushed to give first aid to a Nigerian athlete who collapsed during the long jump.

Diver Alexandre Despatie won a Canadian record nine gold medals between 1998 and 2010.

Island athletes

Many island countries from the Caribbean to the South Atlantic also take part at the Games. The most remote team is probably from the Falkland Islands. At Delhi, Falklanders competed in shooting, **lawn bowls**, and badminton.

SPRINT SENSATIONS

Caribbean sprinters have often dominated the track at the Commonwealth Games. Jamaican athletes won the men's 100 metres in 2006 and 2010. However, the biggest name in Jamaican, and world, athletics has not yet raced at the Commonwealth Games. Will Usain Bolt race in 2014 to beat the 100-metre Games record set by Trinidad's Ato Boldon in 1998?

Jamaica's Trecia Smith won the David Dixon Award for outstanding performance at Delhi 2010. As well as winning the triple jump for the second time, the trained physiotherapist also helped the Jamaican medical team.

United Kingdom divided?

At the Olympic Games and World Championships, athletes represent Great Britain. The **Commonwealth** Games gives sportspeople from Scotland, Wales, Northern Ireland, and England the chance to compete against their Great Britain teammates.

Some British athletes will be hoping that the Commonwealth Games can bring a grand finale to their careers after success as World and Olympic Champions. For others, the Games are a chance to establish themselves on the world stage. Scottish athletes will have an opportunity to succeed in front of a home crowd.

Swimming star Hannah Miley and other Scottish athletes will be proud to compete in the Commonwealth Games in their own country.

Double Olympic champion Mo Farah could challenge the Kenyan dominance of distance running at Glasgow 2014.

ATHLETES TO WATCH FROM FOUR NATIONS

- Adam Gemili (England): The young sprint star will be hoping to build on his 100-metre gold medal at the World Junior Championships in 2012.
- Michael Jamieson (Scotland): The swimmer is likely to be a big favourite with the Glasgow crowd following silver medals at Delhi 2010 and the London Olympics in 2012
- Becky James (Wales): Track cyclist James will be looking to add to the bronze and silver medals she won as a teenager at Delhi 2010.
- Katie Kirk (Northern Ireland): The young 400-metre runner was one of seven promising athletes from around the UK who lit the Olympic flame in 2012.

Disability at the Games

Sport for athletes with a disability has a special place at the **Commonwealth** Games. The Games were the first major sporting events to include disability sports, or **para-sports**, as full medal events. At Glasgow 2014, 22 events for disabled athletes will take place alongside the events for non-disabled athletes.

Visually impaired cyclists compete on tandem cycles alongside a sighted cyclist.

PARA-SPORTS IN 2014

Glasgow 2014 will include events in five different para-sports: athletics, swimming, powerlifting, **lawn bowls**, and track cycling. Track cyclists will compete at the Commonwealth Games for the first time.

Para-sport classification

Para-sports are organized in different classifications so that athletes compete against others with similar levels of disability. For example, athletes with **cerebral palsy** will compete in the men's 100-metre T37 race.

COMMONWEALTH FACTFILE: MANCHESTER 2002

- 3,679 athletes came from 72 countries, competing in 281 events
- Most gold medals: Australia
- 20 countries sent athletes to compete in 10 para-sport events.

The stadium built for the 2002 Commonwealth Games has since become the home of Manchester City Football Club.

Side by side

The Commonwealth Games only include a small number of para-sport events, so many stars of the Paralympics will not have the chance to compete. However, the opportunity to perform alongside non-disabled athletes helps to introduce more people to the amazing skills of disabled athletes.

Welcome to Glasgow 2014

On 23 July 2014, athletes from across the **Commonwealth** will celebrate the opening ceremony of the Commonwealth Games at Glasgow's Celtic Park.

Venues new and old

The sporting venues will include new facilities such as the Sir Chris Hoy **Velodrome**, named after the great Scottish cyclist. Some of Glasgow's most famous sporting **arenas** will also take part. Ibrox Park, home of Rangers Football Club, will host the **rugby sevens** competition.

Badminton will be played at Glasgow's Emirates Arena.

Glasgow has a long industrial history but the modern city is a centre for art, culture, and sport.

For 11 days, a total of 14 venues will host sporting legends alongside young athletes in their first Commonwealth Games. There will be amazing sporting successes, celebrated with the friendship and joy in competing that have always been a part of the Commonwealth Games.

Gold rush

The tourist beaches of Australia's Gold Coast are very different from historic Glasgow. But the thousands of athletes taking part in the 2018 Commonwealth Games will still be hoping to bring a gold medal home with them.

ATHLETES' VILLAGE

Games organizers have to think about more than just the sporting venues. An athletes' village in the East End of Glasgow will be home to 6,500 athletes and officials during the Games. After 2014, the buildings will be converted into housing for local people.

Commonwealth Games factfile

COMMONWEALTH SPORTS

The **Commonwealth** Games programme is made up of ten core sports, which feature at every Games, and up to seven optional sports.

- Core sports: aquatics (swimming), athletics, badminton, boxing (men), hockey, **lawn bowls**, netball (women), **rugby sevens** (men), squash, weightlifting
- Optional sports for Glasgow 2014: cycling, gymnastics, judo, shooting, table tennis, triathlon, wrestling

Most successful countries at Commonwealth Games

This **medal table** includes results from 1930 to 2010.

Country	Gold	Silver	Bronze	Total
Australia	803	673	604	2080
England	611	612	613	1836
Canada	437	460	494	1391
India	141	123	108	372
New Zealand	130	189	245	564
South Africa	104	102	106	312
Scotland	91	104	160	355
Kenya	71	58	66	195
Wales	52	76	107	235
Nigeria	50	55	71	176

Source: Commonwealth Games Federation

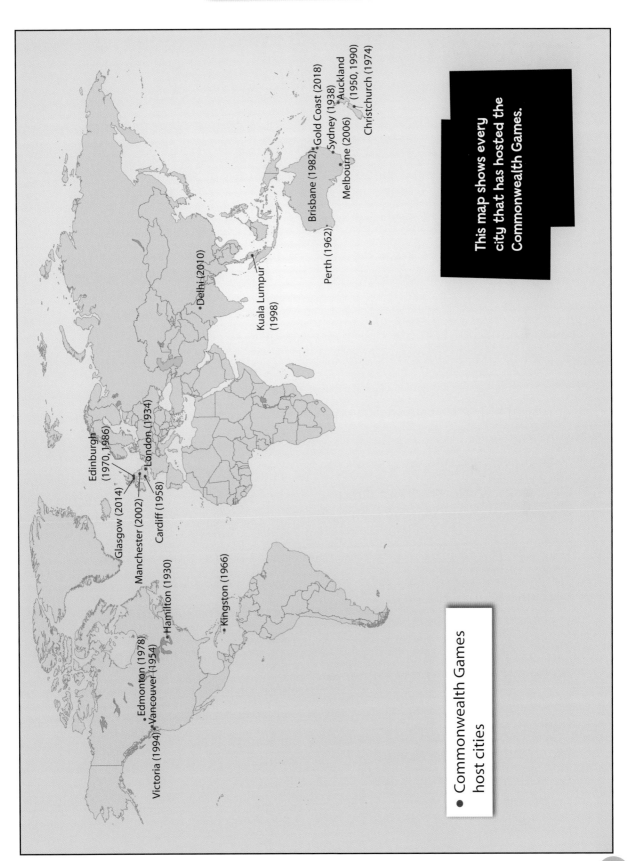

This map shows every city that has hosted the Commonwealth Games.

Delhi (2010)

Kuala Lumpur (1998)

Brisbane (1982)
Gold Coast (2018)
Sydney (1938)
Auckland (1950, 1990)
Christchurch (1974)
Melbourne (2006)
Perth (1962)

Edinburgh (1970, 1986)
London (1934)
Glasgow (2014)
Manchester (2002)
Cardiff (1958)

Hamilton (1930)

Kingston (1966)

Edmonton (1978)
Vancouver (1954)
Victoria (1994)

● Commonwealth Games host cities

Glossary

apartheid system of government that existed in South Africa until 1993. Under apartheid, people of different races were kept apart and the rights of non-white people were restricted.

arena place where a sporting or entertainment event takes place

budget amount of money that you expect or are allowed to spend on something

cerebral palsy condition affecting the brain that leads to problems with movement and co-ordination

Commonwealth organization of 54 countries with shared aims and values, linked by a shared history as part of the British Empire

corruption illegally paying or receiving money to get what you want

democracy form of government in which people vote to choose their leaders in elections

independent when a country is independent, it has its own government and can manage its own affairs

lawn bowls sport in which competitors roll balls so they stop as close as possible to a smaller ball

medal table table showing which countries have won the most medals at the Commonwealth Games

oath promise

para-sport sporting event for people with a disability

patron person who supports a charity or special event

rugby sevens type of rugby union played by two teams of seven players each

velodrome banked wooden track used for track cycling

visually impaired having a disability affecting the ability to see, such as total loss of sight

volunteer person who agrees to do something, usually without pay. Major sports events rely on many volunteers to make them happen.

Find out more

Books

Athletics (Great Sporting Events), Clive Gifford (Franklin Watts, 2011)

Know Your Sport series, Clive Gifford and Paul Mason (Franklin Watts, 2011)

Sport: From Ancient Olympics to the Champions League (Timeline History), Liz Miles (Raintree, 2011)

The Sports Book, Ray Stubbs (Dorling Kindersley, 2011)

Websites

www.thecgf.com
The official website of the Commonwealth Games Federation, which is in charge of the Games. The website includes details of every Games and competing countries.

www.glasgow2014.com
This is the best place to go for information about the Glasgow 2014 Commonwealth Games.

For the 2018 Games, go to www.goldcoastcity2018.com.

www.commonwealthgames.org.au
This is the website of the Australian Commonwealth Games Association. Visit websites for individual countries to find the latest news on teams and athletes.

Index